JOSEF DOYLE

BUSINESS OF ONLINE WRITING

**The Ultimate Guide to Article Income System, Discover
How You Can Earn A Regular Income From Article Marketing**

Descrierea CIP a Bibliotecii Naţionale a României
JOSEF DOYLE
   BUSINESS OF ONLINE WRITING. The Ultimate Guide to
Article Income System, Discover How You Can Earn A
Regular Income From Article Marketing / Josef Doyle –
Bucharest: Editura My Ebook, 2020
   ISBN

JOSEF DOYLE

BUSINESS OF ONLINE WRITING

The Ultimate Guide to Article Income System, Discover How You Can Earn A Regular Income From Article Marketing

My Ebook Publishing House
Bucharest, 2020

TABLE OF CONTENTS

INTRODUCTION TO ARTICLE MARKETING

There are a few important ingredients to creating high performance Article Marketing campaigns that maximize the overall effectiveness of your marketing efforts, while ensuring that you receive the most exposure possible from each article that you submit into the online directories.

First, writing an article on just any topic isn't going to yield the results you're looking for, if you haven't first conducted keyword research to identify what your target audience is actively looking for, and the exact keywords and phrases they are using to be able to locate content on your topic.

This is fundamentally one of most critical elements of a successful article marketing campaign.

The closer you are able to target your prospective customer base with well written articles that incorporate primary keywords, the more traffic and exposure you will be able to generate.

Think about the possibilities if you carefully evaluated a niche market, creating keyword swipe files of highly relevant terms and phrases and incorporated them into your content. Not only will this help you position yourself within the search engines, but your visitors and readers will be exceptionally targeted!

It all begins in researching and evaluating potential markets prior to creating your content.

In the next chapter, we will cover quick-start keyword research as well as how to quickly identify whether a market is a profitable one or not. This will help us focus on spending time focusing only on the topics and niches that will yield the best results.

CHOOSING YOUR TARGET MARKET

There are many ways you can go about evaluating potential keywords and keyword phrases to use within your article content, and with a simple short-cut strategy, you can conduct all of your keyword research in less than 15 minutes.

Before we can begin to locate profitable keywords however, we need to focus on the topic of your articles.

- ✓ What market do you plan to cater to?
- ✓ What products are you planning to promote?

If you are unsure how to come up with a list of hot topics that have a variety of existing products that you can promote as an affiliate, or create yourself if you are able, you can use the marketplace available at www.ClickBank.com to browse existing products that are categorized by popularity.

Clickbank is **the most popular marketplace** of digital products online and has a great selection of products for you to promote. It is essential that you know how to pick products and how to promote them.

If you pick a poor converting product or promote them in the wrong way, you will be wasting a lot of your time and effort.

Visit http://www.Clickbank.com

Conducting market research is a critical part of becoming a successful article marketer if you intend on promoting affiliate based products.

You need to place a severe focus on four critical elements to researching any niche market:

1: Whether there are *desperate buyers* in the market who are eager to purchase a "solution" to an existing problem.

2: The *size of the market* (how many buyers are currently purchasing products or services within this niche)

3: Existing *competition within the market*. (You want competition, it means a viable and active market, however you need to ensure that the competition isn't so thick that you will struggle to penetrate it)

10

4: *Quality and Quantity of the products* in the market (you want to focus on markets that are evergreen and offer an abundance of products to promote in your article marketing campaigns.)

Click on the 'Marketplace' link to load up the categories and search options.

Once inside of Clickbank's marketplace, enter in keywords or keyword phrases that describe the niche that you are interested in.

If you aren't sure what topic to begin with, you can simply browse through the most recent products that were added to the ClickBank marketplace, or search through existing categories.

You will notice that with Clickbank, each product listing features specific information regarding its current stats.

Here is what these mean:

- **$/sale:** The amount of money you earn for each sale.

- **Future $:** Average rebill revenue.

- **Total $/sale:** Average total $ per sale, including all rebills.

- **%/sale:** The percentage of the product sale price that the sale represents.

- **%/refd:** Fraction of publisher's total sales that are referred by affiliates.

- **grav:** The measure of how many affiliates are promoting the product.

For each affiliate paid in the last 8 weeks Clickbank adds an amount between 0.1 and 1.0 to the total. The more recent the last referral, the higher the value added.

The Gravity indicator will tell you how well a product is selling. So a gravity score of 100 means a product is potentially selling better than one with a gravity score of 20.

Focusing on what is currently selling will make it exceptionally easy to come with ideas for your own products, as well as what topics to write about.

Note: From within the ClickBank marketplace, if you click on "Create Hoplink", ClickBanks' system will generate an affiliate link that is custom and assigned only to you. You will need to create a free ClickBank account prior to being able to generate an affiliate link for specific products.

Start by writing down a few topics from the marketplaces that are currently in demand. With each topic you write down, create your hoplink and copy and paste that into your text file so that you have it when it comes to creating your landing page.

Spend 30 minutes or so browsing through ALL of the categories on ClickBank. Don't just pick one or two, but try to create a list that encompasses products from all different genres and niche markets.

Finally, you should end up with something that looks like this:

Water To Gas

Hoplink: http://your_id.water4gas.hop.clickbank.net/

Satellite TV for PC

Hoplink: http://xxxx.ipodpsp.hop.clickbank.net/

Truth About Six Pack Abs

Hoplink: http://xxxx.mikegeary1.hop.clickbank.net/

You need to dominate each product you promote within the article directories.

You do this by having MORE articles than your competitors. So to recap. Let's review what we learned.

1. **Find a product to promote that shows interest**. It is fine if you do some keyword searches before time to practice, but your first priority is finding a product.

2. **Conduct multiple keyword searches** to find out what search terms people look for when searching for the product you plan to promote.

3. **Make sure the product is HOT NOW**. You can do this easily by visiting the Clickbank marketplace, which ranks products according to how well they sell. If you find a product you like, but it is at the bottom of the list, or has a bad sales page, do not bother moving forward.

Find a product to promote before you even think about keyword research.

Make sure the product is hot right now, which is easy to tell on Clickbank, which is why I recommend it, make sure it has a good sales page and the sales page is working fine, make sure it offers fair commissions and make sure also that the owner is contactable.

What is a decent commission? If someone is really interested in getting their product to move, they are going to offer affiliate commissions of at least 50% (that is 50% of the sales price) to get you to promote their product.

Some will offer a lot more than that. If you can find a high paying affiliate product, one that sells for a good price and offers a commission of 70% or more, you are golden.

All you have to do is dominate the market by creating great articles and saturating the entire market with fresh, high quality content.

For every product you find that you want to promote, you should write 20 articles. You should be able to get 20 articles out a day.

So in 5 days, a working week, you would have 100 articles written and have 5 Clickbank.com products promoted and saturated.

When you have decided what niche markets and/or products you are going to promote, it's time to complete your keyword research so that you can create articles that offer a blend of high quality content, with relevant keyword phrases.

If you are planning on promoting a specific product, you should also consider integrating both the product's title and the author's name into some of the articles in your campaign, so that you can pull in targeted leads from those searching for information on these products.

If your articles end up being based on a review platform, where you offer detailed information regarding specific products, you will be able to tap into an exceptional customer base of hungry buyers already on the verge of making the purchase but just needing a bit of reassurance.

To begin evaluating potential keywords, visit: https://adwords.google.com/select/KeywordToolExternal

What you need to do is enter in a basic (core) keyword phrase that describes your market, topic or a product you are planning to promote. (example: product title, author's name, etc.)

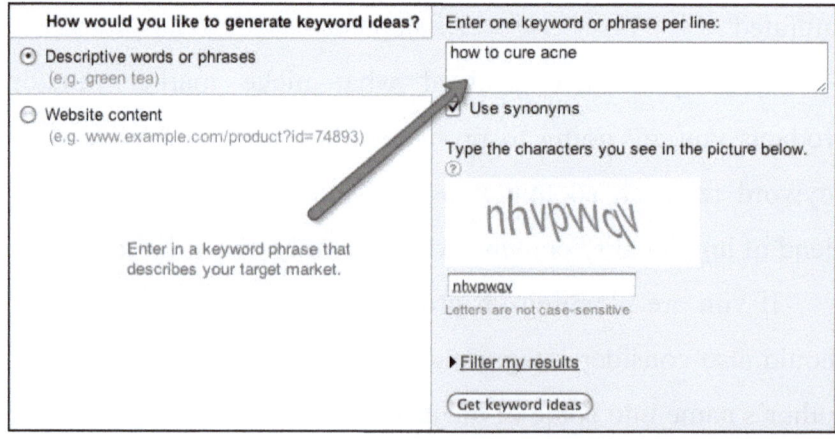

The Adwords Google Keyword suggestion tool allows you to enter in a keyword or phrase from a possible niche that you are considering so that you can evaluate existing competition, active keywords based on popularity and overall use.

When you enter keywords into the Google Keyword tool, you will be able to generate extended listings that feature various keywords associated to the main keyword that you entered into the search box.

Keyword		Searches	Competition
how to cure pimples		880	1,900
how to treat acne		9,900	9,900
how to clear acne		8,100	6,600
how to prevent acne		5,400	4,400
acne pimples		9,900	8,100
acne home remedy		14,800	12,100
clear acne		74,000	40,500
acne treatments		110,000	110,000
how to get rid of pimples		27,100	12,100
getting rid of acne		8,100	8,100
pimple cure		2,900	3,600
pimple treatment		6,600	12,100
cure pimples		4,400	6,600
cure acne		90,500	74,000
acne scars		201,000	135,000
acne remedies		74,000	60,500

The first column provides you with alternative keyword phrases that you could use within your content as well as with search engine optimization or promoting your product within PPC marketplaces.

The second column indicates the level of competition, and in our example above, nearly all of the featured keyword phrases appear to be heavily targeted by existing competitors, including Adwords (PPC) marketers.

The third column indicates the estimated number of searches for each particular keyword, based on monthly volume.

Keyword research can take a bit of time when you are first starting out, but as you become more experienced with choosing relevant keyword phrases and weeding out the ones that are likely to be ineffective, you will be able to create entire keyword swipe files quickly and easily, each time you develop your article marketing campaign.

Here are a handful of other free keyword tools and resources:

http://www.KeyCompete.com

http://www.Wordtracker.com

http://www.Compete.com

http://www.SEODigger.com

With the KeyCompete tool, you are able to extract keyword lists from those used by your competition within PPC marketplaces and campaigns.

You are also able to instantly evaluate the popularity of a specific keyword phrase based on the number of websites that feature these keywords within their website's overall content.

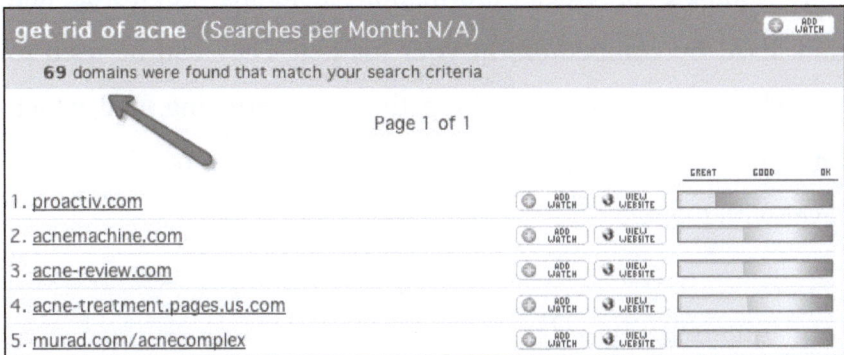

Here are some other useful sources for locating new topics on subject matter that people are currently looking for information on:

http://trends.google.com

This website will display the popularity of specific search terms and phrases.

If you enter in a keyword such as "Dog Training", it will show you exactly how many people are searching for that specific term. You can use this tool to determine how popular a niche market is, as well as how common certain keywords are.

http://www.Compete.com

Compete provides information including keywords and rank used by competitors in your market. They can be used to tell which keywords your competitors are targeting, and which ones they are ranking for. This can help you compete on a new level with them

http://answers.yahoo.com

This is a great way to locate common questions that people are seeking answers to.

Not only can you register a free Yahoo Answers account and answer open questions, (including your website link within the source box), but you can quickly browse common trends on topics that people are interested in.

Once you have a list of niche topics and subject matter that you plan to write about, you will need to ensure that your articles are written so that they are not only sensible to someone reading them but that they are crafted to rank as high in the search engines as possible.

www.WordTracker.com

WordTracker is one of the most well-known and popular keyword tools. Its results aren't the most accurate in terms of traffic numbers, but it does give you a wide variety of keywords.

It is said that you should multiply the numbers it gives you by around 3-10 to get an accurate reflection of the total number of searches on Google, or on all major search engines.

The paid version will allow you to get unlimited keywords at a time, but they also have a free version available at http://freekeywords.wordtracker.com that will give you 100 keywords at a time.

Another quick way to evaluate the level of competition for various keywords is by using the major search engines and directly entering in your keyword phrase, as shown below:

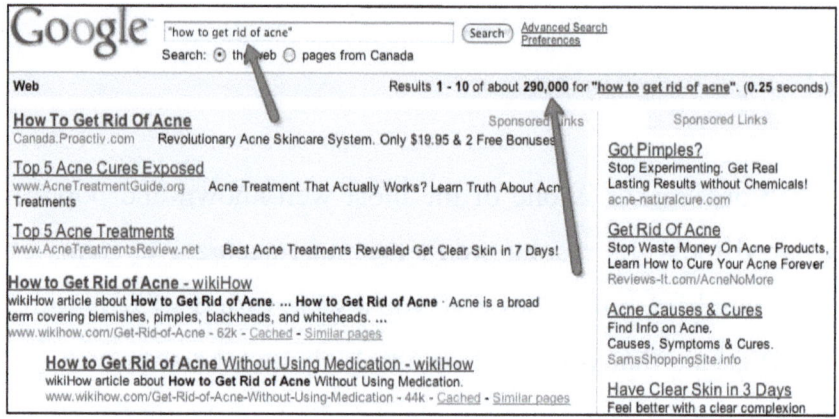

The phrases you should target in the beginning should ideally have fewer than 150,000 results in Google when you search for them in quotes, like this. "Keyword phrase here".

Overall, article marketing is exceptionally easy and with a few short-cut methods you can also reduce the time required in creating and distributing your articles.

YOUR ARTICLE CASH MACHINE

To begin, let's open an Ezine Articles account, in the event that you don't already have one. If you do, that's great – however there will be a few small tweaks and changes that you will need to do in order to optimize your Ezine Articles account for best preformance.

While Ezine Articles (otherwise known as EA) manually approves each article, once you have been approved for your first ten, you may be given what is referred to as "Platinum Status". With Platinum status, you are able to submit an unlimited number of articles.

Let's go over to Ezine Articles and create our account . http://www.EzineArticles.com

You will be asked to fill out a registration form that includes your email address, choice of password, your first and last name as well as your address.

Make sure that the information enter into the registration form is valid, as Ezine Articles can terminate your account for failing to provide updated information.

If you have any problems during the registration process, Ezine Articles provides a video tutorial guide on their site that you can review for assistance.

Once you have finished, the first thing you will want to do is fill out your authors profile and add a photo if you have one.

Ezine Articles allows you to add a couple of links to your resource box, however for best results, I would suggest focusing **only on one website per article.**

You want to avoid confusing your reader or making it difficult to know which website to visit, especially when they are seeking specific information relating to your article content.

One way of going about this is to create multiple resource boxes, featuring one website link and brief description within each. You can then selectively choose which resource box to use with each article that you write.

Once you have finished, the first thing you will want to do is fill out your authors profile and add a photo if you have one.

Once you have set up your account, enter your email address and password into the login form to access your account details.

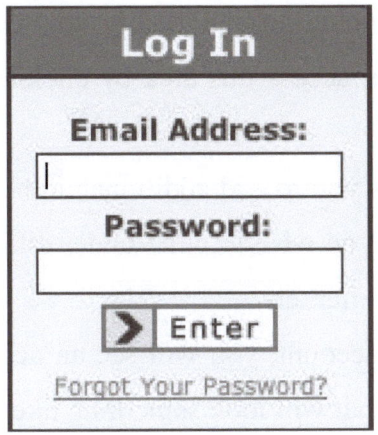

From within your administration panel, you will be able to submit articles and once you have a handful of approved articles, you can check for current stats including article views, ratings (that visitors have left you based on whether they felt the article was high quality or not), and even what articles are ranking higher than others.

You can access this information from within the drop down menu under "Author Tools" .

As your account begins to feature more and more articles, these statistics will become invaluable in helping you focus on creating high converting articles that generate interest and subsequently, traffic to your websites, while weeding out the ones that simply aren't working.

There are many other features available to you from within EzineArticles admin panel, including the ability to add an author's resource box. You can access this area by clicking on the 'Profile Manager' tab.

Ezine Articles also allows you to add additional authors to your account, in the event that you wish to write under different pen names, catering to multiple markets.

When you log into your account, you will see an account overview on the left hand side that will look something like this:

Account Statistics	
Article(s) Views:	3,732
Profile Views:	180
Articles Published:	120
URL Clicks:	102
Emailed:	1
Comments:	1
Votes:	13
Live Articles:	55

This box shows how many articles you have that were approved and are "live" (visible), as well as how many times your articles were viewed, how many times your profile was viewed, how many clicks were generated as a result of your articles and more.

The URL clicks are important. This is how many times someone clicked a link within your resource box and since the primary objective is to encourage your readers to visit your landing pages or websites, the higher the number of clicks, the better your articles are performing.

If you aren't sure how to structure your articles, or what kind of articles are performing the best, spend some time evaluating existing articles throughout the different categories on EzineArticles.

Look at other people's articles and see what they've written about. Find out what people are searching for on the Web using tools like the selector tools at overture.

What you are doing is basically rewriting other successful articles. Now, you are not PLAGIARIZING. Instead, you are creating original material, but **referencing** the work of others for ideas so you can create a better article.

Your job is essentially that of an article re-writer. Every article topic imaginable has been written for you at Ezinearticles.com. There are millions of articles listed here, and all contain links or resource boxes to other people's affiliate sites or information.

Take advantage of this system, exploit it and rise above your competition. It is the simplest way to get ahead in the industry.

Read an article, and then write your own article. Fill in the gaps. Find out what benefits you need to include the original author didn't mention. Don't copy, create an original work. Just make it unique, different and better than the competition's existing material.

It's that simple.

Remember, you do not have to create a best-selling article. You are not an expert writer at this point, and you may never aspire to be.

You want to do it quickly and easily.

Practice Increases Speed. The more you write, the faster you will get.

Force yourself to sit down and write and not move until you have 4-5- articles done every hour.

If you spend more than twenty minutes writing any one article, you need to improve your speed. You should be able to create 300 word articles in less than 15 minutes after a few days, and if you first create your swipe file of topic ideas, you will be able to increase your speed easily.

First, go to:

http://www.ezinearticles.com

Search for articles on the topic you want to write about. When you find the articles, scan them quickly. Do a quick search for keywords.

Then churn out five original articles based on the information you find. Congratulations, you are on your way to becoming a successful bum marketer. Now, how long did that take you?

With practice, it will take you ten minutes or less to write an article. It may not happen overnight, but it will happen, this much I promise.

Why I say this is because the article marketer with the most articles out there getting hits and traffic is going to win.

To win, you don't need the best articles, you need the highest **QUANTITY OF ARTICLES.**

Understand this.

YOU DO NOT need to be the most prolific writer out there to win. YOU NEED TO WRITE THE MOST ARTICLES.

The more articles you have, the more articles people are going to read. The more articles people read, the more click-through links you will get, and the more money you will make.

That is how the system works.

When writing your articles, use simple, everday words. That way you won't confuse your reader and you will encourage them to read your entire document. Quite simply, you want to offer quality information in as concise a way as possible.

No fluff. One or two pages of hard-hitting good information and you will enter the winner's circle before you know it.

If you are able to outsource the writing to a seasoned writer, even better!

That will free up your time to create landing pages and improve your website so that when these visitors arrive, after reading your articles, you are able to convert them into a subscriber or a customer.

Here are a few freelance marketplaces that will help you get started in finding the perfect writer for your niche markets.

http://www.Guru.com

http://www.WriterLance.com

http://www.GetAFreelancer.com

http://www.Scriptlance.com

http://www.eLance.com http://www.Constant-Content.com

In any event, it's important to submit articles on a frequent basis, in fact, if you can get into the habit of writing one article a day, and submitting it into the leading directory, EzineArticles.com, you will begin to see traffic in no time at all.

Another thing to keep in mind is that if you outsource your content you should use the same writer or a similar writing style within the articles AND the landing pages that you direct your readers to. People tend to prefer specific styles, and you need to ensure that the place you are leading them to uses the same style and theme. You need to be consistent!

Personally, I use the services at

http://forums.digitalpoint.com

to locate pre-written article packages on my target market.

Since Digital Point offers a free marketplace where writers can post their content for sale, it's an affordable and super quick method of gaining access to pre-written articles on any topic imaginable.

In fact, it should cost you no more than $20-30 for a package of 10 articles (which is enough to start submitting into the article directories).

SETTING THE WHEELS IN MOTION

Now that you have chosen your topics, products, and have compiled your keyword lists, you're ready to create and submit your articles into the online directories.

In truth, choosing your initial markets and products to promote is a large chunk of the work involved, and now all you need to do is write (or outsource) a handful of articles focusing on these specific topics.

Specific being VERY important.

First of all, you need to ensure that your article directly connects to the product or topic that you are promoting.

Do not write a great article about parenting and then provide a link to a product selling weight loss tips. You NEED to closely tie your article with a specific topic, product or focus.

When writing your articles, keep them slimmed down to only 300-400 words in length. We want to keep them short and on track, remembering our objective is to entice them to read the entire article and then click on the links featured within our author's resource box leading either to a landing page, squeeze page or direct to the merchant's website after being tagged with our affiliate link.

If you struggle to come up with topic ideas for your articles, one easy strategy is to use the 'number technique' which incorporates a bullet list into your document.

Example: ' Ten Tips To Saving Money At The Pump', or 'Top Five Methods Of Minimizing Acne'.

There are three parts to every article. Let's take a look at what these are, and how you can make sure yours are written in the best possible way.

Article Title

The first thing your reader will see is your article title, so it's an exceptionally important part of your article and serves as a headline does on a salespage.

Your title needs to captivate them, get their attention and prompt them to read further. You want your article title to be irresistible so they can't help but click on the link and read the entire page.

Article Description

When article directories submit your content into their database, typically your title shows and possibly your description, or the first paragraph within your article content.

This is one of a few reasons why that first paragraph is so important. It not only works to describe what your article is about, but just like the title or header, it also needs to work to motivate your reader to continue reading.

Article Body Content

The remainder of your article should carry the reader right to the end. Don't think that if your title and initial paragraph is good that they will simply continue reading, you still need to bring them along with you by weaving your article content so that it directly addresses the topic of your article.

Keep it interesting and on topic. Use short paragraphs rather than lengthy ones and limit your article body content to 400 characters in total.

With your article, you need to:

✓ Use a clear and direct title that captures attention instantly.

✓ Follow it up with the first paragraph clearly describing the topic of your article.

✓ Continue with the body weaving a story, and doing its job by keeping the visitor reading through to the end.

✓ The closing paragraph or statement satisfying the reader with an ending to the story if you choose that style and prompting them to read the resource box below.

✓ The resource box then compels the reader to click on a link by offering free information in the form of a free report, ebook, video, tutorial, ecourse or something else, relevant to the topic of your article.

To solve the problem of how to write an article that doesn't give away too much or not enough, there is a very simple system that works every single time.

It looks like this:

1) **Topic Introduction**

2) **Examples Of Subject Matter**

3) **Solution / More Information On Subject Matter**

With the topic introduction you are clearly explaining exactly what the article is about. If you were writing about how to quit smoking, you would explain the benefits of quitting, the available aids and so on.

Then, you would provide examples that directly relate to your topic, for example with smoking, you could provide examples of some of the remedies or aids that don't work.

And finally, you would provide information on a possible solution, and show them exactly how to get started.

You also want to try to stay within a 400 word guideline. Articles that are too lengthy will only distract your reader.

The opening paragraph is one of the most important elements of every article you write, as this is the first few seconds in which you will either capture their attention or lose them forever.

CREATING A COMPELLING RESOURCE BOX

When it comes to creating your resource box, you need to spend time evaluating the best strategy for effectively using the minimal space that you are given.

With most article directories, an author's resource box can onlybe a few lines in length, meaning that you have very little space (or time) to motivate your reader to click on your links and visit your external websites.

Your author's resource box is the ONLY element of your article that allows for promotion, so it's vital that you create a compelling resource box that invokes a call to action and entices every reader to follow through by clicking on your links.

With sites like Ezine Articles, you are able to create multiple resource boxes, choosing one that compliments each article that you write. You can also create multiple author's accounts so that you can cover a large number of topics, all within one account.

Use your resource boxes wisely, and make sure that you offer your reader with an incentive to click through.

One way of doing this is by offering a free giveaway in your author's resource box that is relevant to the topic or market that your article is focused on.

If you are not sure what you can offer within your resource box, here are a few things I have used successfully for over a year now:

❖ **Free Report**
❖ **Newsletter or Ezine subscription**
❖ **Free ebook**
❖ **Free sample of a paid product**
❖ **Free Trial Membership**

When creating your author's resource box, make sure to use anchor text whenever possible. This will help you rank for specific keyword phrases within the search engines.

While not every article directory permits anchor text within author resource boxes, whenever possible include various keyword phrases pertaining to your market.

You also want to incorporate a strong call to action, directing your reader to click your link and explore your website.

Here is an example of a great resource box:

****

Shelby Morris specializes in teaching bloggers how to make the most money possibls regardless of experience or skill.

To gain instant access to all of her widely profitable blog tools collection where you can learn exactly how to generate income from your website instantly, click the link below now!

http://www.your-site.com (leads to squeeze page with a free report on profitable blogging)

****

You should also limit the number of links contained within your resource box to only one, so that your reader is given a clear message, to click on your link and visit your site, rather than being confused with multiple options.

Your overall article should tie in with the website that is featured within your author's resource box.

For example, if your article is focused on acne remedies, you should lead your readers to a squeeze or landing page that offers additional information on how to cure or control acne.

Make sure you keep a strong, clear focus with every article you create, connecting it to a relevant resource box.

QUICK START ACTION PLAN

Follow this action plan every week and you will be well on your way to earning $100 - $200 a day with article marketing and affiliate based products.

Step 1 – Choose Your Products

You need to locate a handful of high quality products to promote within your articles.

Clickbank.com is a good start to find products to promote. There are new products being added daily, and you can spend time evaluating popularity, gravity and overall performance by using the free resources available at http://www.CBEngine.com and http://www.CBTrends.com

Make sure that you are being adequately compensated for your time and effort. Don't promote a product that pays you less than 50% commissions.

Another great idea is promoting residual income affiliate programs.

Example: Hosting accounts where you are paid on a recurring basis for each person you refer to the hosting provider.

If you want a list of some good affiliate programs that pay on a recurring basis, here is a quick resource:

http://www.lifetimecommissions.com

Step 2 – Compile Your Keyword Lists

Start with at least 25 keywords per topic so that you have a swipe file available whenever you create your articles.

Focus on incorporating the product titles, author's name and extremely relevant keyword phrases that will attract readers and ultimately, customers.

Step 3 – Write or Create The Articles

Once you have chosen your products, defined your keyword lists, it's time to create the articles for submission. The more articles in circulation, the more exposure you will receive.

Make sure that your articles are of high quality, relevant to the market or overall focus, and speak directly to the reader.

Try to create at least 10-20 articles on each topic or product that you intend to promote.

Step 4 – Create Landing Pages And Submit Articles Consistently

Create high converting landing and squeeze pages by enticing your reader to subscribe to your mailing list in exchange for a free giveaway (ebook, report, etc.).

Add these links to your author's resource box and incorporate a strong call to action to motivate your reader to leave the article directory and explore your website. Remember, articles are meant to drive in traffic, NOT to sell. If you capture their information and focus on building a massive targeted mailing list, you can always contact them with future follow ups.

This is pre-selling at its best. Many people really hate giving away their email address straight away just to get more information, so give it to them free repeatedly, and they will eventually WANT to give you their email address.

There is already too much junk mail out there, so more and more people want something tangible immediately. Make sure to write up your initial follow up email after signing up for a professional autoresponder account (I recommend either www.Aweber.com or www.GetResponse.com)

Once you have created your landing page, submit your articles MANUALLY to Ezinearticles.com and Goarticles.com, as well as other popular article directory sites (see resource section at the end of this book for more information)

Step 5 - Double up on your keywords

By now you should have written a large number of articles and submitted them to the relevant article directories. If after a few weeks, you find a certain product is doing really well, double up.

Always keep on top of your article marketing campaigns to determine what articles are performing and which ones need to be tweaked, modified or removed entirely.

Use the resources available within your article marketing accounts on sites like www.EzineArticles.com that will help you evaluate your overall efforts.

Keep moving ahead! Article marketing is all about consistency!

CONCLUSION: FINAL WORDS

Create your article marketing system and work on it every week, so that you are able to reach out to new readers ensuring that your content is in constant circulation.

When it comes to article marketing, quantity is just as important as quality. The more articles that you have in circulation, the more traffic (and potential sales) you will be able to generate from all of your submissions, however you also want to focus on submitting only high quality, well written articles.

Remember, you are not only using articles as a way of generating targeted traffic but in developing a brand, or in building brand awareness if you are a new marketer or developer.

Remain Consistent! In order to maximize the performance of all of your article campaigns you need to stay consistent, adding fresh new content into your article directory accounts, ensuring that your campaigns retain their exposure while you keep the momentum going!

Never let a campaign lag. Instead, focus on submitting 3-4 articles a week, either personally written or outsourced by high quality freelance writers.

Always spell check your articles and ensure that they are easy to read and are broken up into paragraphs. Make sure that you communicate directly with your reader by first researching your market, and identifying with the types of products and content your prospects are searching for.

Create squeeze and landing pages that will help you utilize article marketing as a way of building targeted lists of subscribers. That way, you can send out broadcasts and future follow up emails with additional affiliate products as well as an equal balance of fresh, high quality content.

Article marketing is a fun and effective method of gaining mass exposure and driving unstoppable traffic to your websites, while building a list, furthering a brand or developing a reputation in a brand new market.

Take action and work towards consistently expanding your outreach with an ever-growing number of articles in circulation, and you will be leaps and bounds ahead of your competition.

9 786069 837238

Printed by Libri Plureos GmbH in Hamburg, Germany